Friendship Quilts

Marieke Dijkers

Introduction 4
The history of friendship quilts 4
Organising a friendship quilt 5
Appliqué quilts 9
Developing an appliqué pattern 12
Requirements for appliqué 16
Templates 20
Appliqué 24
Quilting 28
Conclusion 32

Kangaroo Press

All beginnings are difficult
Jet Meijer, Irnsum, Friesland

Quilt: 176 x 220 cm (69¼" x 86⅜")
Block: 30 cm (11¾") square
Border: long side—1 cm (⅜"), 9 cm (3½"), 12 cm (4¾"), 6 cm (2⅜")
short side—1 cm (⅜"), 9 cm (3⅜"), 4 cm (1¾"), 6 cm (2⅜")

Before making our friendship quilt Jet had always made quilts by the pieced method where small pieces of fabric were sewn together by sewing machine.

She had never considered making an appliqué quilt before. She thought that working together with her Pearl friends using self-designed blocks would be rather a challenge. She had one bed in her house that really needed a quilt. It was a very beautiful old grey wooden cot that had been used by Jet's father when he was a small boy. When her parents had moved house the cot had been given to her and it was just crying out for a beautiful quilt.

Jet chose a blue background which accentuated the Dutch checked, striped and floral fabrics used as appliqué. The flying geese in the border were made from the same fabrics but were sewn together. With this decorative quilt for a cover, the cot has become a feature in the guest room used by her grandchildren.

Dream roses
Yke Castelein, Jorwerd, Friesland

Quilt: 200 cm (78¾") square
Block: 30 cm (11¾") square (25x)
Border: 1 cm (³/₈"), 8 cm (3"), 15 cm (6"), 1 cm (³/₈")

Yke had been dreaming for a long time about a rose garden. A rose garden filled with all sorts of rose bushes—standard roses and cottage roses in shades of red and pink with yellow centres. These rose dreams have become a reality in her original quilt design called *Dream roses*.

She has now decided that the robust conifers in her front garden will have to be moved to make way for roses. The log cabin quilt on her bed is also going to be replaced by *Dream roses*.

The Pearl friends have each appliquéd one dream rose and four hearts for Yke. All her friends have been represented in this quilt; each one has donated one heart that has been worked into the border. The outside border has been made to look like a picket fence around the rose garden. It has become a very charming quilt, totally fulfilling Yke's dream.

Introduction

My Pearls, formerly members of the Dutch Association of Flatlands Women (similar to a Country Women's Association), have been meeting together annually since 1981. Each year a new quilting or patchwork technique is discussed and examined and a new project is taken home by each member to complete.

A newspaper headline, 'There is Not Enough Togetherness', drew my attention. It inspired me to try a new direction. In consultation with my Pearl friends we decided to try making friendship quilts for each other. We would experiment with a technique we had not used before, and it was unanimously decided to try appliqué quilting.

We worked out our own formulae for doing this and set aside two years for completion of the quilts. In this publication you will see the system we used and the results we have achieved. We are all very happy with our appliqué friendship quilts and have a visible symbol of more than fifteen years of friendship together.

I am very proud of my Pearl friends and it is easy to see why when the quilts are displayed. When you read how simply we started this project, inspired by shapes and forms in nature, you will become inspired also. Naturally I hope that you will feel inspired to organise a friendship quilt, perhaps with a different system, for yourself, a good friend or a special occasion. You will enjoy the feeling of togetherness.

Marieke Dijkers

The history of friendship quilts

Many appliquéd friendship quilts were made in America between 1840 and 1860. In the sparsely populated areas of the country there was a great need for social interaction. Families were spread far and wide and needed each other desperately. In the winter, quilts were a necessity as well as very attractive items of decoration.

Practicality and self-expression together made quilting an important creative outlet. The activity gave quilters a feeling of great satisfaction as well as enjoyment. Working together on friendship quilts was an opportunity for people who otherwise would not have met to make social contact. The expression 'quilting is sharing' means that not only are the patterns, scraps of fabric and ideas shared, but also the many joys and sorrows of life.

Getting together to make the quilt was usually done to mark a special occasion, such as when departing friends were travelling to the west coast of America, possibly never to meet their old friends again. Quilts were often made for the bride and groom as well as for important people like church leaders, teachers and doctors. Some quilts were made to mark important political events.

Friendship quilts form a separate category in themselves and are available in six different variations.

1 Album quilts
These are appliquéd masterpieces and have usually been made by a group of twenty-five, thirty or forty people. Album quilts were the first of the classic friendship quilts that were made in different parts of America, circa 1840. Each was made to its own recognised pattern using the traditional colours from that particular area.

2 Wedding quilts
These were usually appliquéd with hearts, garlands of flowers and love birds (Figure 1). They were made for the bride and groom, to wish them well and keep them safe from harm.

3 Friendship quilts
These are usually made from a less involved pattern and are appliquéd or sewn from small pieces of fabric (pieced quilts). A combination of these techniques can also be used.

4 Freedom quilts
These quilts were usually made by young unmarried girls for young men. The mother or sister of a young man would invite the girls to make a freedom quilt. The girls would be very happy to come and would bring their own scraps of fabric with them.

The quilt would be presented to the young man either on his twenty-first birthday or at his graduation when he had completed his training. The quilt stayed in his possession until he met the girl he was to marry, at which time it was presented to her.

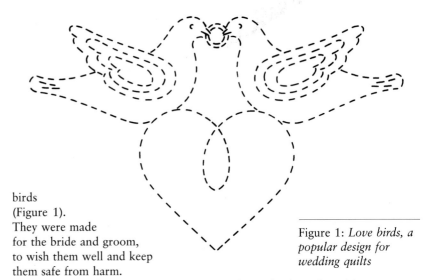

Figure 1: *Love birds, a popular design for wedding quilts*

Obviously, the girls wishing to attract his attention would have done their very best.

5 Presentation quilts
Presentation quilts were made by the female members of the church community. When a much-loved cleric and his wife departed the community, they were given a presentation quilt as a farewell gift. These quilts are recognisable by the repeated religious symbols and the bible texts written in ink on the quilt.

6 Autograph quilts

Quilters collected autographs from important people such as state leaders, church leaders and generals. They would write a letter to the person asking them for their signature and sometimes for an old necktie to be worked into the quilt.

Adeline Harris Sears (born circa 1863), a quilter from Providence in North Carolina, collected 360 genuine signatures for her quilt from important people of that time. Her quilt even included the signature of President Lincoln.

Signature quilts were also made to raise money for the works of the church. A signature quilt made by Mrs Margaret Culberson from Atlanta consisted of 810 signatures. She had charged ten cents for each signature. The signatures were copied and transferred in ink onto the quilt by Jeff Pierce; the total monies raised were donated to the church. Some quilters not collecting quite as many signatures would ask for twenty-five cents per signature (that amount was a lot of money at the time), but the signature was then very carefully embroidered onto the quilt. There were some families which would pay to have the name of every member of the family embroidered on a quilt, with the proceeds going to the improvement of the church.

Autographs are still collected by many people, but I have not come across any modern quilts with the signatures of today's prominent people. Maybe autograph quilts will make a return to popularity one day.

Friendship quilts are always dated and signed, so they can achieve historic significance with time.

Friendship quilts can also have Bible texts, poetry, rhymes or sayings displayed on them, such as:
'When this you see,
Oh pray for me',
or
'Forget me not',
or
'Roses are red,
Violets are blue,
Sugar is sweet,
And so are you.'

An old Netherlands verse goes:
'The roses have faded,
The lilies have died,
But our friendship
Will last forever.'

In the centre of an old presentation quilt is written:
'Presented to Mrs Reed
as a token of affection
by the ladies of the 2nd
M. E. Church, Williamsburg
Through Mrs H. Maujer
May 1846'

These are all lasting memories with a very personal touch from a certain period in the life of a person. They will be treasured by the owner of the quilt for many years to come.

The classic friendship quilts from the period 1840 to 1860 were the precursors of the diaries of the

Figure 2: *Friendship quilts were the origins of autograph albums*

Victorian era, which reached the market in approximately 1870 (Figure 2). These diaries are still sold in one form or another to this day.

Organising a friendship quilt

The principle behind the friendship quilts in this collection works this way: twenty-two quilters as well as myself each designed one block for an appliqué quilt. This design was copied twenty-two times. One copy, together with detailed instructions, was sent to each member of the quilting group. Each member subsequently made twenty-two different blocks and returned each finished block to the original block designer. This way each member received twenty-two blocks of her original design, but constructed by the other members of the group. Each member made their blocks into a quilt and then completed the quilt to her own specifications.

Starting a friendship quilt, as with any other quilt, will require a certain amount of preparation. A lot of thought, communication and planning are needed to get it off the ground. Communication is essential for success. Organise at least one, possibly two, social get-togethers with all the members of your group. Make an unanimous choice on a project, or take a majority vote if

Figure 3: *Make a list of interested quilters. Keep a note of any extra information that could be useful*

necessary. Any decision must be put in writing, so that each person is totally aware of the whole picture. Even with written instructions, things will not turn out exactly as planned. This is one of the most interesting and surprising elements about organising a friendship quilt.

Hints to help the organisation:
- The best way to start a friendship quilt is to make a list of people who may be interested in joining in (Figure 3). Note their names, addresses and contact numbers.
- Leave enough space to add important notes such as: 'I'd like to help but...', ' I am only available on...', ' I can help with stretching quilting...', etc.
- Involve as many people as possible in a friendship quilt so each person feels part of the project, creating a feeling of unity.

Tulips from Flevoland
Jeltje Kramer, Dronten, IJsselmeerpolders

Quilt: 190 x 220 cm (74¾" x 86⅜")
Block: 34 cm (13⅜") square (20x)
Border: 24 cm (9½"), 3 cm (1¼")

In winter Flevoland is endlessly flat, bleak and grey, but when the tulips announce the start of spring and the fields of bulbs come out in blooms, there is a festival atmosphere in Flevoland.

Jeltje wanted to make a quilt with lots of tulips. As the tulip is a rather symmetrical flower, she wanted to bring a bit of life to her pattern; she achieved this by rotating each of the leaves a little to the right.

Each member of the group made four tulips and was given pieces of the same green fabric to ensure that all the leaves in the quilt would match. The border was made by Jeltje and consists of a garland of tulips. Jeltje finds quilting a very relaxing experience, and there is not an area of more than 1 cm (⅜") square on her quilt that has not been quilted.

In the centre of the quilt where the blocks meet, Jeltje has added twelve exquisite tulips using a trapunto technique. The amount of quilting that has been done on this particular quilt has given the fabric a totally different texture, making it a truly unique treasure.

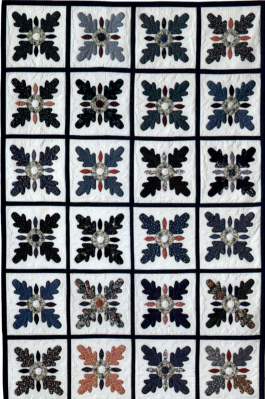

Garden party with the Pearls
Meta Blok, Prinsenbeek, Noord-Brabant

Quilt: 200 cm (78¾") square
Block: 30 cm (11¾") square
Border: 10 cm (4") floral fabric,
         15 cm (6") plain blue fabric

Meta thought the idea of working out and making each others' appliqué patterns was a fantastic idea. Her vision was a garden party with fantasy flowers made by her Pearl friends. With asymmetric fantasy flowers placed in the centre of the block, she has conjured her friendship quilt into an enchanted garden party. According to Meta there were many different creations possible with her design, but this is the result. The border is made from twenty blocks. The centre of the quilt consists of four blocks made into a diamond. Four large white triangles and a sculpted strip bring the block back to a square. That Meta enjoys quilting can be clearly seen by the gridwork and the self-developed flower motif within.

Meta still cannot believe how beautiful her quilt has turned out. Her man, who is not usually generous with his compliments, said without any prompting, 'That is very beautiful' and that means a lot to her.

Oak leaves
Ati van Veenendaal, Tholen, Zeeland

Quilt: 151 x 225 cm (59½" x 88¾")
Block: 34 cm (13³⁄₈") square (24x)
Border and strips: 3 cm (1¼")

Ati had planned to choose as simple a pattern as possible. The pattern had to be plain to allow the fabrics to dominate. Her choice became the classic pattern of four oak leaves in a garland. This is a much-loved basic pattern. Using folded leaves, she cut the pattern to the required size. She asked each of the Pearls to choose a fabric for the oak leaves with a lot of blue and a small amount of red in it.

Ati sent a piece of fabric for the centre with all her patterns to ensure the continuity of her quilt. It suited Ati better to quilt the appliquéd blocks first, before she stitched them with strips of blue fabric 3 cm (1¼") wide. This is called the 'quilt-as-you-go-method (see Figures 48–53). In the large oak leaves, the veins in each leaf have been quilted and the leaf pattern has been quilted around six times. This is called echo-quilting (see Figure 45). The back of the quilt is white, but through the echo-quilting the oak leaves make a beautiful pattern on the back of the quilt.

- Invite a number of people together, explain your ideas and vision and give everyone a chance to put forward any ideas they may have. Let everyone return at a later date with a completed design, where a choice can be made or a vote can be taken, with the majority approval.
- The completion date will need to be clearly stipulated. In practice there will always be people who are late, so it is advisable to allow an extra fourteen days for completion. This will prevent disappointment. Consult your list of names and refer back to the comments.

Using these as your guide, organise more meetings to get together and complete the quilts. If the friends live too far apart it is possible to organise for the quilt to rotate every fourteen days. Make a roster, remembering to keep everyone involved to achieve the true meaning of a friendship quilt.

Designing a friendship quilt

- Determine the size of the quilt first, to prevent it getting out of hand (Figure 4). You will need graph paper or a handy quilter's ruler, which can be used in four different scales (1:2, 1:4, 1:8 and 1:5). Start by measuring the total size of the quilt onto a piece of paper, using a scale of 1:8. Subtract the size of the border. The area that is left can be divided into a number of square blocks (Figure 5).

How large will I make my quilt?

Figure 4: *Determine the format of the quilt first, then make the divisions.*

- Choose a suitable base fabric for the pattern; plain white or a similar fabric is suitable for this.

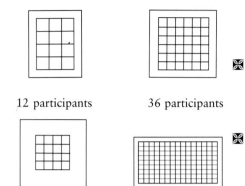

12 participants   36 participants

16 participants   135 participants

Figure 5: *Not only can you vary the format of the quilt, but also the size of the blocks and the width of the border.*

Figure 6: *Write clear instructions next to the pattern and glue some examples of fabrics as well*

Tear the fabric into strips and cut the squares from the strips.
- Use extra seam allowance for this base fabric; 3 cm (1¼") would be sufficient. This is especially necessary because the fabric may fray or you may need to square up the base fabric after the block has been appliquéd.
- Friendship quilts are usually made from simple patterns to enable everyone to join in, so it is best not to make the pattern too intricate.
- Choose a main colour that suits the person for whom the quilt is to be made. Remember that the main colour will need to be used for the border as well as the centre of the quilt. The colours that are used by the friends do not necessarily need to be the main colours, but they should be matched to the wishes of the person making the quilt. An instruction such as 'do not use black but use dark blue', or 'do not use white, but an off-white' should be respected.
- Spend extra time on your text describing the method and any other instructions necessary to make the block. This can save many questions later, as the response to mailed blocks is naturally larger.

Our oral instructions were as follows:

- Design an appliqué quilt with a motif of flowers or leaves, using examples from potplants or the garden. Use a photocopier (see page 12).
- Using a fine pencil, draw your

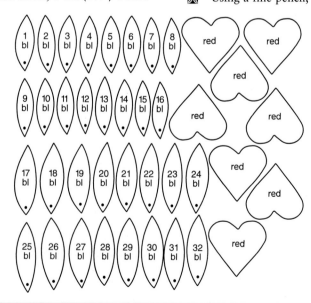

Figure 7: *Draw all the parts on freezer paper*

pattern onto a cotton base fabric or draw the points for the pattern.

- On paper give clear and complete directions for the person who is about to make up your design. Make sure the directions are not confusing (Figure 6).
- Draw all the parts of the design onto freezer paper (Figure 7).
- From your scrap basket add two or three pieces of fabric, but not all the pieces as your friends will need to add pieces from their scrap baskets too (Figure 8).
- Make one complete package with clear instructions for each of the twenty-two Pearls and send these packets by mail to each person (Figure 9).

When all the Pearls and myself had completed the above instructions, we each received twenty-two different packages in the mail. We were given exactly one year to appliqué the twenty-two packages with their different contents. We were filled with curiosity and were dying to know how the twenty-three quilts would look when they were finished.

One year later when everyone met again for the second time, each person was returned their original packages, but now the squares were appliquéd as well as having been provided with a signature. We decided to take an extra year to join all the blocks, make a border and quilt the resulting coverlet.

At the third meeting all the quilts were handed in. This was quite an event for all of us. All the quilts were hung and each person told their own stories about their quilt. Sadly, there were two Pearls who through unexpected circumstances at home had been unable to finish the quilting. This is the reason that there are only twenty-one quilts in the book instead of twenty-three. The number of blocks used in the twenty-one quilts also differ. In some cases extra blocks had to be added, whereas in others some of the blocks have been used in the back of the quilt. In this book you will find the results that our organisation of friendship quilters delivered. Beside each friendship quilt you can read the experiences and stories of the quilters, giving the quilts an identity of their own.

We celebrate this educational appliqué friendship arrangement which has taken two years to complete, with the publication of this book; a testimony to our fifteen years of friendship as a quilting club.

Appliqué quilts

It goes without saying that each quilter in his or her life will take the risk and make an appliqué quilt. Appliqué is like painting with small scraps of coloured fabric. All sorts of free shapes are possible—you are not bound by geometric shapes such as squares, rectangles and triangles. The main difference between an appliqué quilt and a pieced quilt is that the small pieces of fabric are sewn onto one larger piece of fabric in an appliqué quilt, while a pieced quilt involves sewing the pieces of fabric to each other.

These two techniques can reach very different results, even using the same motifs (Figure 10). Creating the appliqué quilt allows the quilter a greater creative freedom—this is often overwhelming—but it is worth mastering the initial hesitation and making the first step towards starting an appliqué quilt. With each attempt to create, using for example flowers and plants from your own garden or windowsill, you will get a find sense of achievement. Most of the quilts in this publication were made in this way.

Figure 8: *From the scrap baskets of the other participants came the most interesting scraps of fabric*

Figure 9: *Send the completed package to the other members of the group*

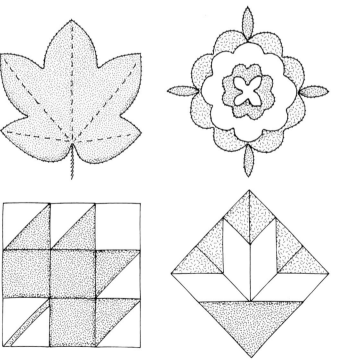

Figure 10: *One leaf and one flower in a pieced quilt and an appliqué quilt*

My Pearl
Corrie van der Kooy, Woudenberg, Utrecht

Quilt: 245 cm (96½") square
Block: 38 cm (15") square (25x)
Border: 27.5 cm (10¾")

Corrie was the only one of the Pearls who had previously studied appliqué quilting. It was a challenge for her to create a pattern for her own design.

As she did not want to make it too difficult for her fellow Pearls, she used her experience and chose large flowers, as larger patterns are easier to make. In the centre of the pattern she placed three berries and four leaves. Strange as it may seem, these small berries and leaves are an integral part of the design. They change the shape of the blocks and give direction to the quilt. If the pattern is placed next to the quilt, the meaning of this becomes quite clear.

The border with all the names of the Pearls and the additional quilting has given Corrie a lot of satisfaction. In her opinion it is similar to reading a good book—she was disappointed when it was finished. She has named the quilt *My Pearl* and with good reason—this quilt is a pearl that will accompany the Kooy family for many years to come.

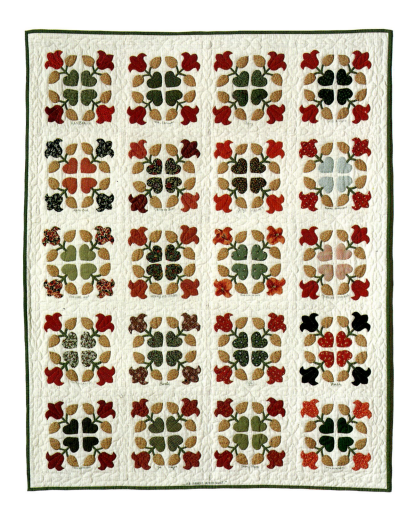

Twenty-three Pearls in one quilt
Nel Berkhouwer, Purmerend, Noord Holland

Quilt: 120 x 150 cm (47¼" x 59")
Block: 28 cm (11") square
Border: 4 cm (1½")

Besides her hobby of quilting Nel is also involved in another hobby—folk art paper cutting (see Figure 17). She wanted to combine her two hobbies in her design *Twenty-three Pearls in one quilt*. A lot of thought was put into the design, with the outcome being that the quilt was to have hearts, leaves and flowers. Hearts symbolising love, leaves for protection and flowers for life.

It was a simple pattern, without quilting problems. Not everyone kept to the chosen colours, as all the hearts should have been green and the flowers a dark red, but the quilt is more interesting with the different colours worked into it. Friendship quilts will always have a certain beauty because of the unusual and individual colours and fabrics that the original designer wouldn't have used. Nel did not make her quilt very large as the quilting had to be done in the few free hours of summer holidays. The Pearls were very special and have a place of honour in her home.

Twenty-three Pearls
Aaf Bakker, Kwadijk, Noord-Holland

Quilt: 110 x 100 cm (43³⁄₈" x 39³⁄₈")
Block: 22 cm (8¾") square (9x in the centre)
22 x 11 cm (8¾" x 4³⁄₈") (12x along the outside edge)
11 cm (4³⁄₈") square (4x in the corners)
Border: 1 cm (³⁄₈"), 10 cm (4")

Aaf has shown that it is possible to make a balanced pattern using just one flower petal in the making of her quilt. The pattern consists of just three identical petals. The two outside petals sit over the centre petal. The pattern and fabric for the centre petal was sent to each member of the group. The Pearls each had to provide matching fabric for the other two petals from their own scrap baskets. The border is made from the same fabric as the centre petal.

Aaf is employed in a specialist quilting shop in Amsterdam with an awe-inspiring collection of beautiful fabrics—little wonder that she found

her inspiration there. With twenty-five blocks from twenty-three Pearls, the quilt was made in the 'quilt-as-you-go' method (see Figures 48–53). At all the intersections of the blocks Aaf appliquéd a 2 cm (¾") circle, instantly altering the visual concept of the pattern. Aaf uses these sorts of visual concepts quite often in her quilts.

Designing an appliqué pattern

When people say they cannot draw and therefore cannot design a pattern, there are three excellent solutions for that problem:

Designing with the help of nature and the photocopier
Nature and the photocopier can take over all the necessary artwork. Nature and the photocopier are a rather strange but ideal modern combination. Use them both to design your own pattern and enjoy the feeling of satisfaction.

Nature has always been a source of inspiration for quilters. The beautiful shapes and colours of flowers and leaves in the garden or on the windowsill spark a wealth of ideas that can be used to design your own quilt pattern. As soon as you start to study nature you will see that each flower and leaf is quite unique, with a shape entirely its own. Similarly, it is not necessary that all the flowers and leaves in a quilt be exactly the same. A quilt can often be more lively if the flowers and leaves are not all the same size and colour.

The chosen leaves and petals can easily be placed in a photocopier to make a replica (Figure 11). Some photocopiers just copy the image, but there are also photocopiers that can reduce and enlarge it. These are a boon to people who cannot draw.

Figure 12: *A design from the photocopier*

Figure 11: *Photocopying leaves to be used for the design*

- Glue as many petals and leaves as possible to a sheet of A4 paper.
- Place it under the photocopier and make a copy. If there are nicely shaped leaves or petals that are too small or too large, these can be cut out, glued to a piece of paper and enlarged or reduced to the required size for your pattern. Continue cutting out all the leaves that seem to be the right size and shape.
- With a pencil draw one horizontal, one vertical and two diagonal lines onto four separate square pieces of paper that are the same size as the total block without seam allowance. These lines can also be folded, but pencil lines drawn with the quilter's ruler (Figure 24) are preferred as the paper will then lie flat.
- You can now start to make the design by moving the copied and cut-out leaves around on the four pieces of paper. Two mirrors placed on an angle can be a fantastic help here. Place two mirrors upright and at an angle against your block. This will allow you to view the result of a number of blocks together. It is worth experimenting with this.

It is clear to see that the quilt made by Tjallie on page 19 was designed using this method (Figure 12).

Designing with the use of a quilter's ruler and kitchenware
With a pencil and the quilter's ruler draw again the lines as previously, one horizontal, one vertical and two diagonal (Figure 13). Figures 14 and 15 show how the pattern of my quilt was made using the quilter's ruler together with plates, dishes and wineglasses (see also Figures 46 and 47 on page 29). Plates were used to make the circles and the wineglasses were used to make the curved lines of the heart shape. The leaf shapes were drawn by hand to the left and right of the circle (see Figure 16).

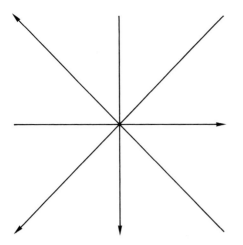

Figure 13: *Using the quilter's ruler draw one horizontal, one vertical and two diagonal lines*

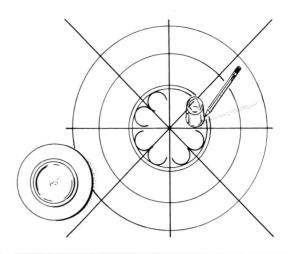

Figure 14: *Draw circles using plates, drinking glasses or a compass*

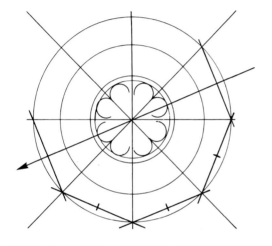

Figure 15: *Connect the points on the circle with lines and find the centre of these lines*

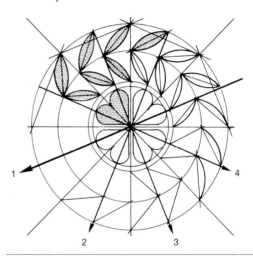

Figure 16: *Draw new lines through the centre point. Draw the hearts and leaves by hand*

Designing with folded paper

You can make beautiful flower patterns and objects using folded paper. This is a very old and popular design method and was called paper-cut-quilts (see the quilt at the top of page 11). Fold a piece of paper double; do this a few times. Cut a shape out of the folded paper. Open the folds and you will have a lovely symmetric shape (Figure 17). A photocopier could be used to enlarge or reduce the pattern to fit the size of the block. It is important make sure the shapes are the correct size, as the design will need to be balanced. Take your time, because while you are busy working on this your imagination will undoubtedly come up with many more good ideas, giving you a multitude of choices.

These are the most basic ways of designing a pattern.

Figure 17: *You can make unique symmetric designs using the folded paper technique*

I love Holland

Marieke Dijkers, Loenen, a/d Vecht, Utrecht

Quilt: 240 x 200 cm (94½" x 78¾")
Block: 40 cm (15¼") square (20x)
Border: 20 cm (8")

'I love Holland, that little country by the sea', sang my mother whenever she was homesick for Holland. I did not understand her homesickness, as I was very happy in the land of the tropical sun where I was born. Now I do understand because I really love Holland. I love the springtime, summer, autumn and winter. I love the area where I live as well as the other provinces. I love the down-to-earth way of the Dutch people, my Pearls—I could not live without them.

The colours of red, white and blue symbolise the glory of Holland to me. With the self-constructed laurel wreaths and hearts and cows in red, white and blue I wanted to express my love for Holland.

I constructed the laurel wreaths with the aid of the compass, a quilter's ruler and some chinaware. After that, the leaves were drawn by hand (see Figures 13–16).

Next to each appliquéd wreath is the name of a Pearl friend, so I will never forget them. Next to the cows are more names; they are the registered names of the cows which are owned by several of the Pearl friends. The patterns have been traced from the book of the calf artist, a dying art; that is why the quilting on each cow is different.

My bridal quilt
Appy Broekens, Gorredijk, Friesland

Quilt: 240 cm (94½") square
Block: 37 cm (14½") square (25x)
Border: 1 cm (⅜"), 26 cm (10¼")

A bridal quilt with self-designed garlands of flowers is what Appy had in mind for her new bedroom with the red timber ceiling. It was many years since she'd been a bride and at that time it was not a custom in the area where she grew up for girl-friends to organise a bridal quilt for their friends.

Appy designed her pattern with a lot of care. The main colour needed to match the timber ceiling, so the large flowers had to be dark red. Appy sent all the members a piece of fabric for the centre of the flowers and lavender-blue fabric for the small bells at the centre of the pattern.

The Pearls added a red fabric from their own scrap baskets to match the centre of the flowers. The connecting branches to the flowers and the border of flowers were appliquéd by Appy. The end result of this basic pattern is a very beautiful quilt. This inspired Appy to decorate the centre of the quilt with extra quilting. The quilt is now on her bed and is the pride and joy of her bedroom.

Requirements for appliqué

- Good quality *fabric scissors* with sharp points (18).
- *Paper scissors* (19).
- *Quilting needles*—'Betweens'. These needles will need to be short and strong. Quilters who have problems with needles breaking would be advised to purchase the original tailor's needles by Leo Lammertz, 'halblange' No. 7 or No. 8; these can be ordered from quilting suppliers (20).
- *Sewing cotton* in a variety of different colours to match the appliqué fabrics used (21).
- *Scale ruler* (21b).
- *Quick unpick* (22).
- *Dressmaker's pins*; preferably short (23).
- *Quilter's rulers*; 30 cm (12") and 60 cm (24") (24).
- *Refillable pencil* HB, 0.5 mm
- *Pencils* that can be used on darker coloured fabrics, i.e. with white, yellow or silver leads (25).
- *Eraser* to remove the pencil marks from the fabric (26).
- *Folding tool* to fold the fabric along the quilter's ruler (27).
- *Template plastic* or *thin but strong cardboard*—This is used to make the templates (see Figure 34 on page 20).
- *Hobby knife* to cut out the templates (28).
- *Freezer paper*—This is paper with a layer of plastic on one side. It is used to cut out the appliqué pieces which can than be ironed onto the fabric. Remember to cut out the pieces

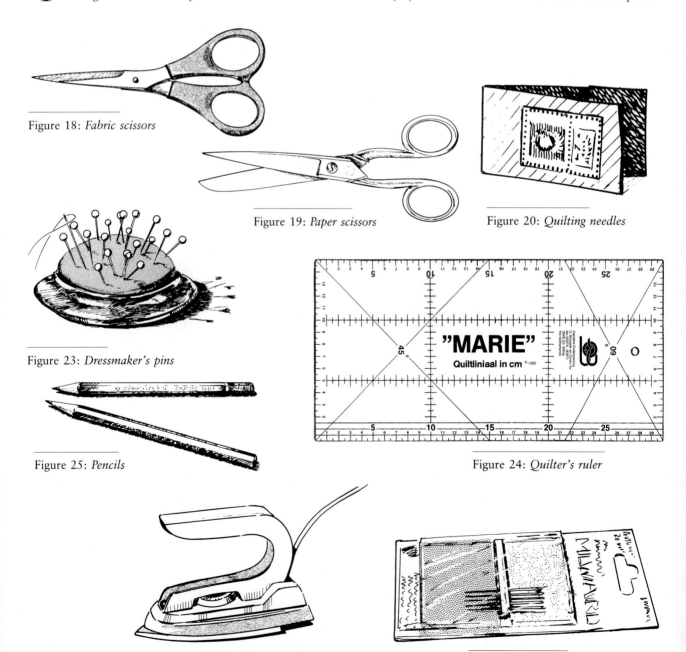

Figure 18: *Fabric scissors*

Figure 19: *Paper scissors*

Figure 20: *Quilting needles*

Figure 23: *Dressmaker's pins*

Figure 25: *Pencils*

Figure 24: *Quilter's ruler*

Figure 30: *Iron*

Figure 31: *Sewing needles*

with a seam allowance. After the appliqué the freezer paper is removed. It does not stain the fabric and is reusable (29).

- *Iron* to press the freezer paper to the fabric (30).
- *Long thin sewing needles*—'Sharps' Nos 10–12 (31).
- *Quilting tool*—This is an excellent quilting aid and preferable to a thimble. It prevents damage to the middle finger and to the muscles of the arm. The quilting tool is held in the same way as you would hold a knife to peel an apple. When peeling an apple the right thumb is placed on the apple. With the quilting tool the right thumb is placed on the fabric (Figure 32). With a little practice this will become a very handy tool to use.
- *Quilting frame or hoop*—This is used to hold the quilt taut while quilting. The rectangular frame offers several advantages over the quilting hoop. The most important of these is that the tension can be regulated by turning the clips which alter the tension over the total length or width of the frame. The frame is demountable and will fit easily into a bag, case or cupboard making it very portable. The rods are interchangeable (Figure 33), allowing six different formations, making three square frames—sizes 43 cm (17") square, 29 cm (11½") square and 21 cm (8¼") square, and three or more rectangular frames of 43 x 29 cm (17" x 11½"), 21 x 29 cm (8¼" x 11½") and 43 x 21 cm (17" x 8¼"). The last size is ideal for quilting the borders. Make sure you read the instructions thoroughly before putting the frames together, or you may end up with broken fingernails.

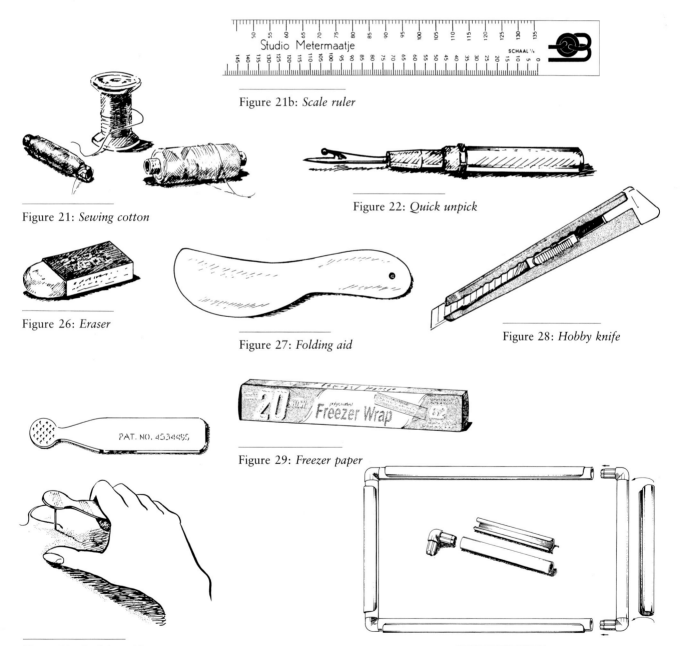

Figure 21b: *Scale ruler*

Figure 21: *Sewing cotton*

Figure 22: *Quick unpick*

Figure 26: *Eraser*

Figure 27: *Folding aid*

Figure 28: *Hobby knife*

Figure 29: *Freezer paper*

Figure 32: *Quilting aid*

Figure 33: *Quilting frame*

String of Pearls
Stien Flipse, Heino, Gelderland

Quilt: 230 cm (90½") square
Block: 40 cm (15¾") square
Border: 15 cm (6")

Stien wanted pearls and garlands of flowers in her quilt, to depict the bond that had formed between the members of this group who had been working together for so long. Some of the members had been together for more than thirty years. It all began with the Netherlands Guild for Flatlands Women.

Quilting has now become a passion for Stien. With pearls, flowers and garlands she has tried to express the bond that holds the Pearls together.

The names of the Pearls are all included on the small purple leaves that have been appliquéd at the crossing of the blocks. Stien had not expected her quilt to turn out as beautiful as it has and she has become very attached to it.

Red berries quilt
Tjallie de Boer, Cornjum, Friesland

Quilt: 185 x 220 cm (72¾" x 86⅜")
Block with berries: 23 x 34 cm (9" x 13⅜") (25x)
Green block: 23 cm (9") square (24x)
Border: 6 cm (2⅜"), 2 cm (¾")

As a child Tjallie lived in Saint-Annaparish, a town with many orchards. The fruit trees were underplanted with redcurrant bushes. In the summer holidays the young people of the town picked the berries, which were manufactured into jam and juice at a local factory. For two weeks of picking berries Tjallie would earn ten guldens, which she then used to pay for one week of summer camp in her own country. Tjallie has had an affinity for berries ever since.

The design of the quilt offered no difficulties because real leaves from the bushes were used for the pattern. The berries were drawn from a template made from a Dutch 10 cent coin. The appliquéd berry blocks have been interchanged with solid green blocks. Everything was so green in Tjallie's past—the berry bushes, the fruit trees and the tops of the great trees surrounding the orchards. The berry quilt has become a wonderful memory of her youth.

This quilt will have a place in the family for many years, together with the personal story of the quilter.

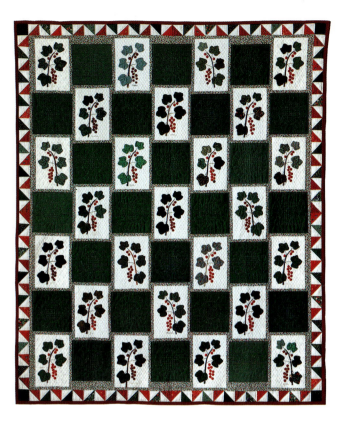

Flower garlands from my garden
Tine Schonenberg, Oldenhove, Groningen

Quilt: 142 x 176 cm (56" x 69¼")
Block: 28 cm (11") square (20x)
Border and centre strips: 6 cm (2⅜")

Tine had always wanted to create a unique design. Asymmetric patterns and uneven numbers had interested her most. Her design, a flower garland, was not divided evenly into 4 parts, but into 5 parts. The result of this is that each of the garlands is rotated slightly. To achieve this effect Tine started by drawing a circle; using a protractor she was able to space the yellow centres of the five flowers at exactly 72°. As a practical exercise she used a large round dish, enabling her to space the flowers in a circle, creating a garland. Nowhere else would you find such a special garland. The Pearls were each given the red fabric for the centre petals. The other two petals were to be made with their own scrap fabrics. Tine was very pleased with the result and was keen to finish the quilting. Around each of the flower garlands are two lines of quilting. The cable patterns between the garlands are formed with three lines of quilting. The back of the quilt is made from a dark green fabric and looks very interesting with the extra quilted lines.

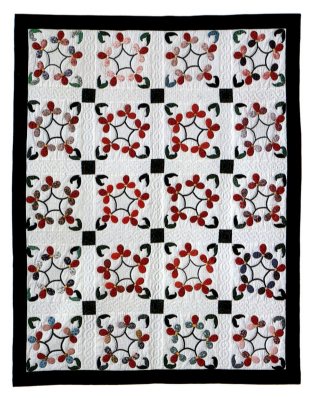

Templates

Templates

The appliqué patterns on the pattern sheet will need to be enlarged by 200% before being transferred onto the freezer paper. If one particular pattern needs to be used more than twenty times, it is advisable to trace the whole pattern onto cardboard or template plastic. This may take some extra time but it is well worth it, because with a template the total pattern can be transferred to the base fabric and each block will be identical in size. The negative template of the whole pattern can be used for double-checking during the appliqué.

Transfer the total appliqué pattern onto cardboard or template plastic. Make sure to mark each individual part, such as which pieces fit together and the colour and the direction of the fabric, before cutting out the appliqué parts with a hobby knife. After carefully cutting out the pattern pieces (Figure 34), you will have two sorts of templates.

- *A negative template:* This is the large template of the total pattern without the appliqué pieces, which have been cut out. This negative template can be used to draw the total pattern with pencil on the base fabric. The shape of the template is drawn onto the back of the base fabric. After being appliquéd, the pieces are sewn together and sewn to the base fabric.
- *A positive template:* These are all the cut-out appliqué pieces. These templates are placed close together on the flat side of the freezer paper and drawn around with a pencil (Figure 7 on page 8). Do not forget to mark and make notations on each individual piece. All pieces are then cut out on the pencil line. The freezer paper templates can be transferred to the fabric with a warm iron.

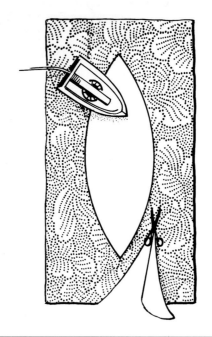
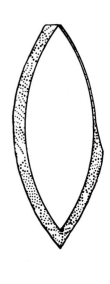

Figure 35: *Freezer paper template on right side of fabric*

Freezer paper—three different methods

There are three different methods to iron the freezer paper templates onto the fabric:

- The freezer paper template is ironed to the right side of the fabric and cut out with a seam allowance of 4 mm ($^3/_{16}$"). This piece is pinned to the base fabric and appliquéd by folding the seam allowance under the fabric and the paper (Figure 35).

  The shape of the paper template is very carefully followed and sewn to the base fabric. The next template can be closely positioned from the indicated contact points, giving a perfect result.

  This method of working also prevents the confusion created by mirror reverse effects. The paper templates are easily removed later and can be used again.

- The freezer paper template is ironed to the reverse side of the fabric, after which the seam allowance is folded over the template and sewn with a running stitch (Figure 36). The part is pinned to the base fabric and sewn to it with small stitches.

  The freezer paper is now between two layers of fabric, which tends to hide the contact points, and makes it less easy to

Figure 34: *Negative and positive templates made from template plastic*

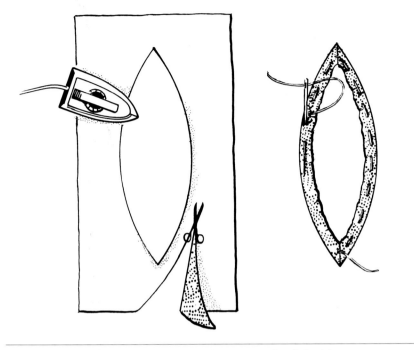

Figure 36: *A freezer paper template on the reverse side of the fabric*

also be glued down with a good quality fabric glue. Do not get confused with the mirror reverse effect here.

All the Pearls and myself chose the first method. It suited us all.

Mirror-reverse effect

This tends to happen with asymmetric shapes (Figure 38). The leaves all have the same shape, but one points to the left and the other to the right. Place a red dot on each leaf so that you can immediately see which side is the top and you do not cut out two right facing leaves.

Appliqué parts with pointed ends

First fold the end of the seam allowance under. Fold one side over the point and then the other side. The seam allowance can be sewn together with a few small stitches (Figure 39). The part can then be appliquéd.

place the next piece against the contact point. By making a small slit in the reverse side of the base fabric, the freezer paper template can easily be removed with tweezers.

When the parts are not symmetrical a mirror-reverse effect can occur with this method. Correct marking of the templates can prevent this.

✠ The seam allowance is ironed onto the shiny side of the freezer paper with the point of the iron (Figure 37). This saves double handling, because the ironed seam does not need to be sewn. The seam allowance can

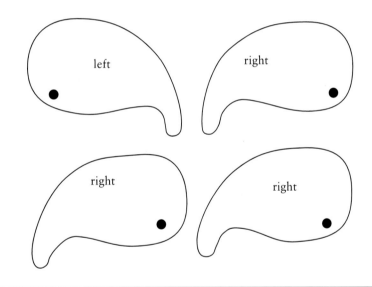

Figure 38: *Mirror reverse confusion*

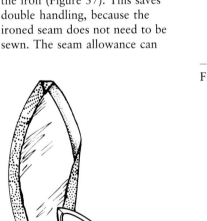

Figure 37: *The seam allowance is ironed to the shiny side of the freezer paper*

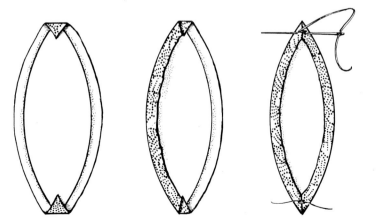

Figure 39: *The appliqué points are completed*

Hendrina
Henny van der Linden, Tollebeek, IJsselmeerpolders

Quilt: 40 x 190 cm (15¼" x 74¾")
Block: 26 cm (10¼") square (24x)
Border: 18 cm (7")

It is not a rose, it is not a daffodil, it is a Hendrina. A very interesting self-designed flower that attracts attention.

Henny constructed her quilt from twenty-four Hendrinas. Henny was enormously pleased with her quilt. Her family were originally not as enthusiastic, but now admit that it is a beautiful quilt. The quilt is unique and distinctive. Is it the quilting, the Hendrina or the design? Hendrina is a Pearl and does her name proud.

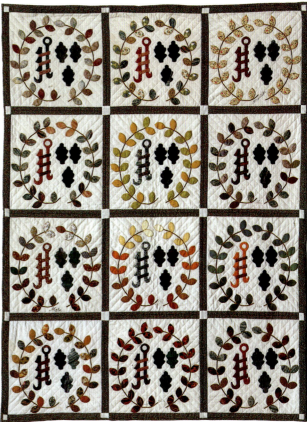

Homan's Shield
Heidi Homan, Gieten, Drente

Quilt: two times 113 x 150 cm (44½" x 59")
Block: 35 cm (13¾") square (two times 12x)
Border and centre panels: 2 cm (¾")

Heidi used her Homan family shield as a pattern for her friendship quilt. It consists of a chimney hook—this is a hook permanently fixed in the chimney above the fire; water kettles and pots are hung on the hook to provide the family with their daily meals and hot water—and next to the hook are three oak leaves with a ring of corn around them. Heidi's two sons were very impressed with their mother's work and as both wanted to have the quilt, she made two quilts. The quilts are hanging beside each other now, but when the boys leave home they will each take their quilt.

The shields were made using the quilt-as-you-go method (see Figures 49–53). Four green strips 3.5 cm (1⅜") wide were stitched to the top fabric. The blocks were sewn by sewing machine, folded to the back and seamed by hand. The small white squares were appliquéd on the corner of each block as an extra decoration. This was Heidi's own idea and a variation on the 'quilt-as-you-go' method, where the quilted blocks are sewn together without the extra panels.

The ears of corn have been linked with DMC embroidery cotton in a small stem stitch. The quilting has been kept very simple and if so desired, the two quilts could be sewn together to make one large coverlet.

Appliqué

Appliquéing small pieces of fabric onto a base fabric can be done in four different ways: with visible stitching, blind (invisible) stitching, by machine or with decorative stitching.

Visible appliqué
This is done by sewing the appliqué piece to the base fabric with even stitches, using a cotton that matches the colour of the piece that is to be appliquéd.

Blind appliqué
This is done with a hem stitch. This stitch is absolutely invisible, because the needle and thread alternately follow the pencil line of the appliqué piece and the base fabric (Figure 41). It is very important to take the thread through the fabric very straight, as when the thread is tightened the stitches close straight against each other.

The thread is hidden in the fold of the seam allowance of the appliqué piece; the straight stitches will be visible at the back of the base fabric.

To prove this: use black cotton to sew a white appliqué piece onto a white base fabric. If it is done properly the black cotton should not be visible. For this method of appliqué the pattern is drawn on the right side of the base fabric and the right side of the appliqué piece. Freezer paper is not used with this method of appliqué.

Perfectionists actually like to match the weave in the base fabric to the weave in the appliqué piece, so that the fabrics both run in the same direction.

Appliqué by machine
Using a zig-zag stitch or another decorative stitch available on a modern sewing machine, the appliqué pieces can be sewn onto the base fabric.

If it is necessary to be very exact with the appliqué, such as with the cows on page 14, it is advisable to use freezer paper. The freezer paper template of the cow was first ironed onto the fabric and then pinned to the base fabric.

Using a small sewing stitch, guide the sewing machine around the outside of the cow. Remove the freezer paper and carefully cut the fabric on the outside of the sewing line with a small pair of sharp scissors (Figure 42).

Then using a fine zig-zag stitch, sew along the line. For a better result, slightly ease the tension on the top of the sewing machine.

Decorative appliqué
Use a buttonhole stitch or a blanket stitch in a contrasting or matching colour to the appliqué piece (Figure 43). This stitch was usually used so as not to waste any of the fabric. The contour of the appliqué piece also gave a decorative effect to the popular buttonhole stitch.

The very old antique quilts adorned with appliqué flowers cut from extremely expensive fabrics were always sewn with decorative appliqué and it is not difficult to see why this was done. These pricey cotton fabrics (brought to the Netherlands by the big merchant ships sailing to the East Indies or Indonesia in the seventeenth century), were printed with the most outstanding decorative floral motifs. The fabrics were highly-prized and their cost made them unavailable to the average wage earner.

From 1680 these fabrics were imported on a larger scale but even to this day they remain costly. These flower motifs were cut out very carefully, without a seam allowance and appliquéd onto a white base fabric with a buttonhole stitch. In this way, a whole quilt could be made from a very small piece of expensive fabric, by grouping the cut-out flowers in baskets and garlands or floral twists. This was called *broderie perse*, but those who could not afford the costly

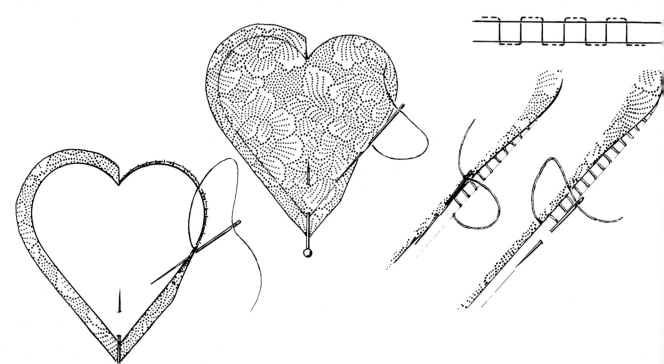

Figure 40: *Visible appliqué*

Figure 41: *Blind (invisible) appliqué*

flower prints thought it was the work of lazy embroiderers. These were actually very beautiful quilts, with much quilting in the white fabric surrounding the appliqué flowers.

The lovely flower patterns on these imported fabrics spurred the embroiderers to action. They embroidered their own flowers which were sometimes even better than the *broderie perse*. This became known as crewel embroidery.

The *broderie perse* quilts were the very first cotton appliqué quilts in Europe. At that time, Europeans knew only of linen and woollen fabrics, which were often quite stiff and difficult to wash. Even today there are no cotton plantations in Europe and the search for alternatives such as viscose, rayon, acetate, nylon and other synthetic materials is on-going. Quilters still prefer to use 100% cotton fabric for their work.

Appliquéing strips

In many of our appliqué designs you will need narrow round, straight or concave lines. All these pieces are made from diagonally cut fabric strips. Pull the strip taut to make a hollow line and press into the strip if you need to make a rounded piece. Pin the strip to the base fabric and lightly press with an iron. This will make it easier to appliqué.

General recommendations for appliqué

- Always wash and iron fabrics before use.
- For the base fabric and the appliqué pieces, 100% cotton of a supple quality is recommended.
- Avoid fraying, stretchy or transparent fabrics. Mixed cotton and synthetic fibres should be avoided, as they very often twist. They can be used if you are prepared to make a lining for them.
- Use a small red sticker to mark the top of each template to avoid confusion and mirror-reverse placing of pieces.
- Use a small piece of sandpaper if the edges of the template are a little rough.
- Do not make the pencil lines on the base fabric too thick. They are removable with an eraser, but the prevention of problems is far easier than their cure.
- Seam allowances for 100% cotton fabric should be 4 mm ($^3/_{16}$"). If the seam allowances are too wide it will be difficult to make curved lines. Cutting into the seam allowance at an angle can prevent this.
- Always start at a corner of the appliqué piece and place a pin at the end of the next corner point.
- The outline of a block is always drawn on the back of the block, not on the front.
- It is not necessary to cut away the back of the appliqué piece. In practice it has been proven that the quilting is not affected if the fabric is left as is. The quilt actually becomes stronger and

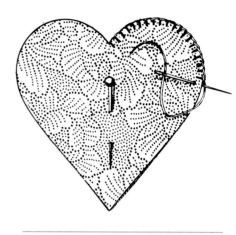

Figure 43: *Decorative appliqué*

more durable if the back has not been cut away. For a quilt that is going to get a lot of use, it is not advisable to cut any pieces from the back.
- Use a very thin needle for the appliqué rather than a quilting needle.

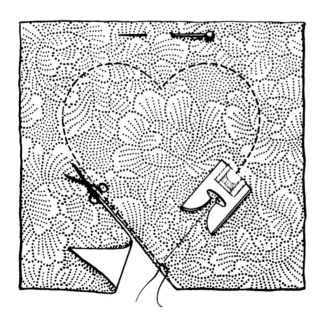

Figure 42: *Machine appliqué*

Teacher's pride
Martha de Vos, Emmeloord, IJsselmeerpolders

Quilt: 240 cm (94½") square
Block with 1 daffodil: 37 cm (14½") square (8x)
Block with 2 daffodils: 37 cm (14½") square (16x)
Border: 27.5 cm (10¾")

With the assignment to design your own quilt from flowers and plants in your garden or window box, a long-held wish became reality for Martha. In her guest room she needed a blue quilt with lots of yellow daffodils. Martha, who has always loved daffodils, did not really understand her appreciation of these flowers until she really thought about it. Every year her third class teacher praised the beautiful daffodils and the very neat garden of her family home, which was a large farm.

Each Saturday it was a chore to rake the gravel paths, but the praise from her teacher made it all worthwhile. According to Martha, this is the reason for her great love of daffodils.

Her design resembles the garden of her childhood home and the intricate quilting symbolises the paths, but it is really too beautiful to represent gravel. Martha has put an enormous part of herself into this quilt, as can be seen in the large open spaces.

The advantage of an appliqué quilt is that the quilting can usually be done very quickly, as there are only a few seams that need to be quilted. The daffodils were not difficult to make and give a very good result.

Tulips from Tine
Berti Saat, Zevenaar, Gelderland

Quilt: 180 x 210 cm (70¾" x 82¾")
Block: 35 cm (13¾") square (30x)
Border and centre strips: 1 cm (³⁄₈")

Berti once received a box of tulip bulbs from a departing member of the country craft commission. Each spring since then, she waits anxiously to see the bulbs come up. What actually happens is that each year more and more bulbs come up. Whenever anyone comments on the tulips, the rest of the family laughingly say 'yes, they're the tulips from Tine.'

Berti wanted to work them into her quilt as a lasting memory. She made an extra three tulip blocks herself. The quilt is made in the quilt-as-you-go method; block after block is quilted and then sewn together (see Figures 48–53). This method of quilting suited Berti, who was not able to handle a large quilt, but was still able to enjoy her hobby. The result was just as abundant as the tulips from Tine in the spring and Berti is well satisfied with her Pearl quilt.

Remembrance and friendship quilt
Willemien Beltman, Laren, Gelderland

Quilt: 156 x 210 cm (61½" x 82¾")
Block: 30 cm (11¾") square (24x)
Border: 18 cm (7")

Willemien kept exactly within the spirit of her assignment by photocopying all the indoor plants of her recently departed mother-in-law. Using the most beautiful of the indoor plant shapes, she went to work and designed this remembrance and friendship quilt. The repetitive pattern of heart-shaped cyclamen leaves symbolises the love and admiration she held for her dear mother-in-law.

The Pearls used the very soft shades Willemien asked for. The names of the quilting friends are surrounded by four hearts and the border is made from overlapping quilted hearts. The pattern is not difficult to make. With just two diagonal lines on the base fabric, all the pattern pieces can be appliquéd one after the other in the right order. For Willemien, this has become a true remembrance and friendship quilt.

Quilting

When all the blocks and the border have been quilted, the blocks can be sewn together either by hand or with a sewing machine. When the top layer of the quilt is finished the middle layer of fibrefill is added and the lining or the back of the quilt is put in place. Together, they form the entire quilt and are then stretched. The three layers are pinned together and then sewn with a basting or running stitch.

Hint: If the lining or back of the quilt is cut 6 cm (2¼") larger than the top of the quilt, it can be sewn to the front of the quilt to prevent the fibrefill from fraying.

Now the quilting can begin. The final work is enormously enriched by the quilting—it brings the quilt to life. A well-stitched quilt always feels very supple and does not crease.

Filling the spaces

There are many different ways of filling the large empty spaces and this is a matter of personal choice. The 30 cm (12") quilter's ruler can be used, with the 45° and 60° markings, to design where and how the quilting is to be done. Figure 44 shows a number of variations for filling the spaces. The lines do not need to be drawn on the fabric before you start to quilt, but can be done as you go along. Use a thin pencil or the folding tool to draw the lines along the ruler. A quilter who really enjoys her task could let her imagination run riot and design all sorts of patterns, from feathers to birds, or hearts, roses and garlands.

Figure 45: *Echo quilting*

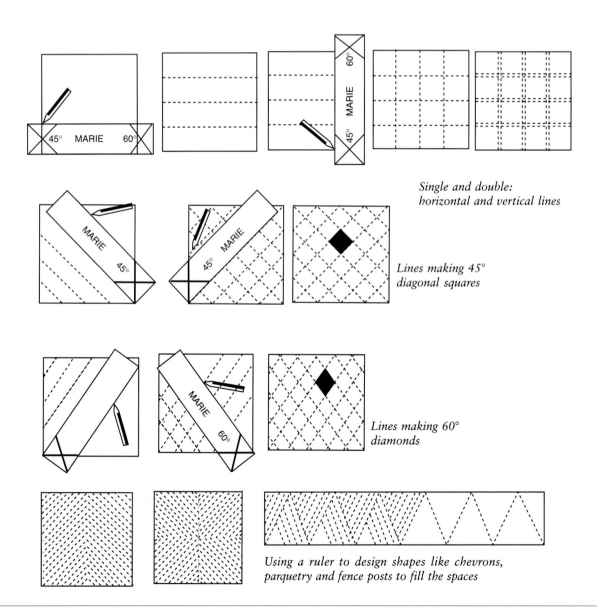

Figure 44: *Using a ruler to make quilting patterns*

Line quilting
In line quilting the pattern is stitched around once, giving a slightly raised effect.

Quilting in the ditch
The stitching is done in the seams, making the quilt stitches invisible.

Echo quilting
In echo quilting, the pattern is stitched around several times until the block around the pattern is filled.

Wineglass quilting
Rub the rim of a wineglass with chalk and twist the circles onto the fabric (Figure 46). This way you can design many patterns, including clamshell and pumpkinseed (Figure 47). Using a silver thimble in the same way, you can make bunches of grapes on the fabric without a pencil.

Quilted borders
Borders are less difficult to make, as they are not usually as large as blocks and are therefore easier to handle. This is obvious from the many beautiful designs such as loops, feathers, cables and spirals that are used to decorate borders.

Finishing the quilt
Use a long quilter's ruler, a roller knife and mat to cut the quilt in one operation. Make sure that both the top and bottom of the quilt are the same size and check both sides as well. If the sides are uneven, decide whether it is possible to cut stitching in the short side, or to add more stitching to shorten the long side.

Cut straight pieces of fabric approximately 6–8 cm (2³⁄₈"–3") wide for the border. Place them on the quilt right side facing, pin them to the quilt and sew with the sewing machine through four layers. Fold the border to the back by hand, and seam to the visible sewing line.

Figure 46: *Wineglass quilting*

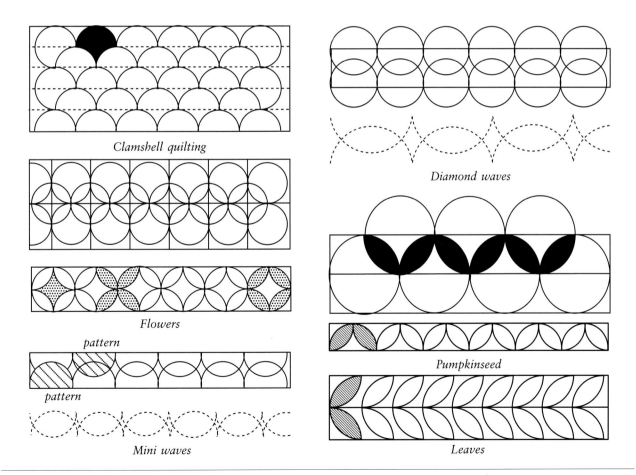

Figure 47: *Different patterns made with wineglass quilting*

A parade of pansies
Nynke Dorenbos, Havelte, Drente

Quilt: 160 cm (63") square
Equilateral triangle: 22 cm (8¾")
(24x pansy without stem, 24x pansy with stem)
Border including edge: 22 cm (8¾")

Nynke has always been fascinated by hexagons, and also by her garden with its multi-coloured pansies. She didn't have to think long choosing the design for her quilt. She wanted the pansies in equilateral triangles—a fitting design for a friendship quilt.

Pansies are easy to make using the appliqué technique. Each Pearl was asked to make two pansies in either yellow, purple or dark red. Nynke drew forty-eight pansies, each in an equilateral triangle. With these triangles she made four stars, the points all touching each other. The plain fabric around the stars was quilted extensively. The border has been made from 116 pansy petals, a very festive border indeed.

Back of My Pearl friends quilt, *page 31*

Pansies for Francine
Trijn Schrikkema, Usquert, Groningen

Quilt: 150 x 200 cm (59" x 78¾")
Block: 25 cm (9¾") square
Border: 25 cm (9¾")

Trijn wanted to make a quilt for her daughter Francine, whose favourite flowers are pansies. While she was drawing the design for the pansy, which is in itself a very decorative flower, she decided she would like to add something to the design. Just as 'pop art' forms are enlarged or blown-up, she decided to make the pansies in each corner larger than life. These very large pansies really give this quilt something extra. The stems and leaves of the pansies in the quilt have all been appliquéd in the fabric Trijn sent out to her Pearl friends. The names of the Pearls are all on the stems, but have been abbreviated, because Trijn can tell by looking at each pansy who made it. Francine will be very pleased with this captivating quilt filled with her favourite flowers.

My Pearl friends quilt
Cock van Leeuwen, Pijnacker, South Holland

Quilt: 124 cm (48¾") square
Block: 20 cm (8") square (25x)
Border: 12 cm (4¾")

Cock was not interested in appliqué quilts, but crying off from her Pearl friends wasn't an option. Inspired by the red and green quilts fashionable in the second half of the nineteenth century, she began work. She decided that her first appliqué quilt need not be very large, and chose the green colours of her farm. The pattern was easily made by moving small circular and heart-shaped pieces around. The red and green fabrics are all totally different; they came from the scrap baskets of the Pearls. When all the blocks were joined together she appliquéd small green circles in the corners of the blocks to give the impression of continuity.

The quilting plays an important role in this quilt and has been carefully chosen. The border has been finished with a houndstooth pattern made from one strip of fabric. The signatures of the Pearls are on the back of the quilt (see the reverse side of the quilt on page 30). Cock now thinks that appliqué can be a lot of fun!

'Quilt-as-you-go'

Some quilters prefer to finish each block separately and then sew all the blocks together (Figure 41). The quilting process is the same, but

Figure 48: *'Quilt-as-you-go', each block is quilted separately*

doing one block at a time means that the work is not so large and heavy. Using this method the quilting can be taken anywhere. In the 'quilt-as-you-go' method, there are two different ways that the blocks can be joined together.

Without strips

The upper layer of each block is pinned together on the pencil line and sewn by machine or by hand (Figure 49). Place the blocks flat on a table with the seams all in one direction. Cut away the excess fibrefill (Figure 50). Be exact when cutting the fibrefill, as the pieces of fibrefill in all the different blocks should join together. The seam allowance at the back of the work is then sewn together (Figure 51). Push the seam allowance to one side. The seam allowance of the upper layer and the seam allowance of the back of the quilt should face in different directions.

In this way join all the blocks horizontally in one row to form a strip of blocks. Then join all the strips of blocks together. The joining of the block strips is done in the same way as joining the blocks, except the strips are longer.

With strips, the faster method

The two blocks, right sides facing, with a strip of fabric placed on the top, are joined together with one seam (Figure 52). Place the blocks flat on a surface and cut the excess fibrefill away. Fold the sewn strip of fabric over the seam and hand-sew this (Figure 53). This is a quick and simple method of joining the blocks. One of the Pearls used the first 'quilt-as-you-go' method, but added different coloured strips between all the blocks. The blocks were not joined to each other, but to the extra strips. As the strips are a different colour they are clearly visible at the back of the quilt. This gives a very interesting effect and makes the quilt reversible.

Figure 49: *First sew the upper layers of the two blocks together*

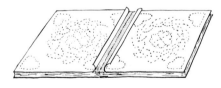

Figure 50: *Lay the blocks flat and cut the fibrefill pieces to join*

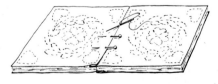

Figure 51: *The back of the quilt is hand-sewn*

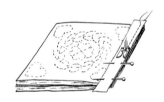

Figure 52: *Two blocks are sewn together with a strip of fabric on top*

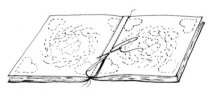

Figure 53: *The strip of fabric is hand-sewn across the seam*

Conclusion

Endless fantasising, making decisions each time, discoveries, problems, finding solutions, making use of given pieces of fabric, matching fabrics when there is not enough and using only what is available, make quilting an interesting pastime. As in earlier days, there is also the necessity for social contact—something every person needs.

I wish to thank my Pearls for their friendship and support. All our quilts have been collected together in this book. It is a visible bond of our friendship, something that we wish to share with other quilting groups and quilters. For us, it was an enormous challenge and the feeling of togetherness has certainly been strengthened.

Bibliography

Bentley Kolter, Jane, *Forget me not: A gallery of friendship and album quilts*. The Main Street Press, Pittstown, New Jersey

Finley, Ruth E, *Old patchwork quilts and the women who made them*. Charles T. Branford Company

Moonen, An, *Quilts, a Dutch Tradition*. Netherlands Openair Museum

Orlofsky, Patsy and Myron, *Quilts in America*. Abbeville Press, Publishers, New York, London, Paris

Safford, Carleton L. and Robert Bishop, *America's quilts and coverlets*. Bonanza Books, New York

Simms, Ami, *Invisible Appliqué*. Mallery Press